EDUCATION FOR ADULTS
AND OTHER ESSAYS

EDUCATION FOR ADULTS
AND OTHER ESSAYS

BY

FREDERICK PAUL KEPPEL

Essay Index Reprint Series

Originally published by:

COLUMBIA UNIVERSITY PRESS

BOOKS FOR LIBRARIES PRESS, INC.
FREEPORT, NEW YORK

First Published 1926
Reprinted 1968

LIBRARY OF CONGRESS CATALOG CARD NUMBER:
68-22103

CONTENTS

EDUCATION FOR ADULTS
AND OTHER ESSAYS

EDUCATION FOR ADULTS
AND OTHER ESSAYS

EDUCATION FOR ADULTS [1]

THE front line troops in our American army of
students make an impressive showing. Stretching
from the nursery to the doctorate, they total, in
kindergarten, in the grades, in high school and
academy, in college and technical school, in the
university, something over twenty-five million
souls. On the whole, the different branches of the
service are pretty well balanced, and if there is not
universal satisfaction as to the leadership on the
one hand and the spirit and performance of the
troops on the other, there is no prevailing weight
of opinion as to what changes should be made, and
the different types of criticism tend to neutralize
one another. The American community is deeply
interested in this army. It recognizes its fundamental importance in the life of the nation, and,
in general, it understands and approves what is
going on.

[1] An article first published in the *Yale Review,* April, 1926,
and reprinted by courtesy of that publication.

So much for the professional educational soldier, the one for whom education is, for the moment, presumed to be the main business of life. How about our militia? How about those for whom educational soldiering, if indulged in at all, must be performed in spare time, for whom learning must be, from the nature of the case, a supplementary activity? When we examine these militia forces, we find a very different situation. We find, first, an almost complete neglect of them and their leaders by our educational general staff. We find a serious lack of balance among the different branches of the service, primarily because recruiting has been encouraged only among those who will pay their expenses — and perhaps turn in a profit. We find no general appreciation of their present number nor of the excellent material included among them; no national realization of their growing importance in view of changing social and economic conditions, nor of their normal place in a well-rounded national life.

This, at any rate, is the impression which the present status in the United States of what we loosely call "adult education" makes upon one who has recently had occasion and opportunity to study the movement rather closely. I wish we had some better term than "adult education" to describe it. It is the process of learning, on the initiative of the individual, seriously and consecutively undertaken as a supplement to some primary occupation. Of course, there is no hard and fast line. Many of the names which are printed to pad the totals of our graduate schools belong to wage-earners who are giving less time, on the whole, to their education than are the men and women in a typical workers' education class. The process obviously may be begun long before the individual can be termed an adult — among the most important questions before us is how to get some effective hold between the ages of sixteen and twenty upon the boys and girls who have drifted away from school. It can be taken up whenever what we call the individual's schooling comes to an end, or at any age thereafter. The start may be made from any rung of our long ladder of formal education. Indeed, one of the first things we must do is to get rid of the idea that adult education is necessarily for the benighted. The clinical classes offered to practising physicians by such institutions as the New York Academy of Medicine, for example, or the classes for engineering executives conducted by Purdue and other state institutions, should be recognized as falling within any adequate definition of adult education.

11

Adult education is no new thing in this country, though we used not to call it by that name. Our grandparents supported the lyceums, and they did their reading seriously. Our mothers, particularly in the smaller communities, were grouped in coteries for mutual intellectual improvement. Its development, as we now understand it, however, has been very recent and, since the war, very rapid. To-day, there are at least five times as many adults, men and women, pursuing some form of educational study as are registered as candidates for degrees in all the colleges and universities in the country. Of course the amount of time which these people can give to their studies is, on the average, far less than that which college undergraduates can devote, but nevertheless the comparison is a striking one.

First in number are the students of the commercial correspondence schools, of which there are about three hundred and fifty in the United States. At least a million and a half new students are registered by these schools every year. A composite photograph, based on a study made last year, pictures the typical correspondence-school student as a young man, twenty-six years old, who has had two years of high school, and has been out of school for ten years. His home is in a medium-sized town of less than one hundred thousand inhabitants, probably situated in a State having a superior educational spirit, Iowa, for example. He is engaged in business or some industrial pursuit, on the semi-skilled plane, and has gone far enough to appreciate the fact that the unskilled worker in all lines is handicapped.

The next group, in total membership nearly a million, includes those in the public evening schools, the part-time and continuation schools. In the evening schools, the lineaments of the composite figure are not preponderantly male as in the case of the students in the commercial correspondence courses. The typical age is nineteen years and six months. Ninety-two per cent of the students are under twenty-four, and seventy-eight per cent are under twenty. On the basis of their own statements, only fifteen per cent left day school because of financial pressure. Most of them evidently left because they had lost interest. Their reason for returning is the realization that education pays. The extent of these efforts of the public education authorities varies greatly from town to town. For example, cities like Milwaukee and Portland, Oregon, can count six per cent of their population in the night high schools, whereas the national average is not more than one and a half per cent. There is also great variation in the numbers of this group in the different States, the South, in general, lagging behind the rest of the country.

About one hundred and fifty thousand students are found in university extension classes, including correspondence courses. Here the composite portrait is feminine; it shows a teacher approximately thirty years of age, studying either English, Romance languages, Education, Mathematics, or History. California and North Carolina are leaders in this type of adult education.

Y. M. C. A. courses number another hundred thousand, with perhaps as many under the direction of other non-academic organizations. Workers' education classes attract thirty thousand.

Turning to less formal opportunities for adults, we find that the various offerings of state and federal agencies in agriculture reach hundreds of thousands throughout the country. In another field, the annual attendance at both the Metropolitan Museum of Art of New York and the Chicago Art Institute, including the concerts, ran, last year, over one hundred thousand, and the aggregate total attendance at other museums of art and natural history probably exceeded this figure. These totals are likely to grow rapidly, for within the past two years more than fifteen million dollars has been spent in the United States in the construction of museums. To these we must add the attendants of the Chautauquas and the lyceums, and the men and women who are following a serious course of study with the help of the local library. We must reckon also with the inaudible spectators of visual education, and the invisible auditors who take their nourishment by radio. How far the newspapers and magazines contribute to what may fairly be called adult education depends on the readers themselves. Probably more people than we realize are acquiring through them the art of being well-informed. All in all, it is certainly safe to say that education for adults has now become one of our major industries.

Our trouble isn't that we have no adult education. Few realize how much of it we have, and how vital and vigorous much of it is.

At the outset of the article I said that our educational militia has been neglected by our general staff, and that there is a serious lack of balance among its different branches. What in plain English did I mean? I meant, first, that this whole vast movement has grown up outside our best educational traditions and leadership, and so without the guidance and control by which it might have profited. There are exceptions here and there, but, in general, this is the situation as it exists to-day. Let me give a single example. The Association of American Universities was founded in 1900 and has had annual conferences since that year. Only once have its deliberations touched the field of adult education, when, in 1910, a paper on university extension was presented; and on that occasion the delegates in their discussion showed much more interest in details of academic book-keeping as to credits than in the possibility of service to the community.

Perhaps the reason for this neglect has been that our American colleges and universities, naturally enough, developed upon the English model, and they have tended to retain certain habits and attitudes which, regardless of how appropriate they may have been for the time and place of their origin, bear no relation to the present situation in the United States, or in England for that matter. Perhaps the most marked of these is the assumption that between Town and Gown a great gulf has been fixed by Providence. In our educational development there have been a few honorable exceptions, notably the University of Chicago from its foundation in 1892 and, somewhat later, the University of Wisconsin. Other institutions were,

16

however, more than cautious in following these examples. Perhaps because of the general shaking up of the academic community which the war brought about, there has been since then much more general evidence of a wider sense of responsibility on the part of the universities and colleges. Even to-day, however, the extra-mural work is largely confined to those very kinds of activity which themselves have been only rather recently admitted to full membership in the academic family — namely, training of teachers, technology, agriculture, and commerce. The present interesting and promising schemes for co-operative courses in which the student divides his time evenly between class-room and shop or counting-house are practically limited to technology and commerce. When we turn to those broad fields of non-technical knowledge which sum up the experiences and aspirations of mankind and which underlie all applied knowledge, we rarely find a really satisfactory offering.

Our steps in the movement for adult education have been limited almost uniformly to those which will pay. Even within the university organization itself, this is true. Extension activities, so far as I know, have never been permitted to draw directly upon the great endowments with which so many of our great institutions have been blessed. In our largest university, the Treasurer's Report for 1924 shows receipts for extension classes of almost a million dollars, and expenditures which do not exceed $650,000. In the stronger state-supported universities, the plan of expenditure contemplates a contribution of five dollars from the student for every seven dollars spent, a much higher ratio than that which the State asks in the case of a regular student. In the smaller state institutions, the policy is to make the extension work wholly self-supporting. All along the line, the development of adult education has been controlled by this economic factor, and I think I am justified in saying that, in the great majority of cases, the enterprise is frankly commercial in character.

Now, what does this mean as to the general nature of the work which is offered? It means, as one would naturally expect, an overwhelming emphasis on vocational courses — courses in which the student can see a quick return for his investment. Among the hundred thousand students in Y. M. C. A. courses, for example, fully three-quarters pursue purely vocational studies — accountancy, stenography, advertising, salesmanship, automobile mechanics, blue-print reading, and other technical subjects. Of the remainder, a majority are at work, not for study's sake, but for credits needed for matriculation into professional schools of law, or dentistry, or pharmacy. The residue, which gives up its leisure in response to an impulse to acquire knowledge for its own sake, is inconsiderable, if not negligible. Between Y. M. C. A. and Y. W. C. A. studies there is a difference only in degree. The somewhat larger proportion of Y. W. C. A. students who pursue non-vocational studies may be explained by the greater cultural interest of the feminine half of the population in all strata of American life. We have already seen that the university extension student is typically a teacher, and it is fair to assume that the fact that academic credits may be obtained towards degrees or certificates, which, in turn, lead to elevation in the educational hierarchy, is a more potent influence than what we used to call the pursuit of learning. In the correspondence classes, ninety-five in every hundred are studying radio telegraphy, engineering, shop mechanics, bookkeeping, or some other subject equally specialized, in the interest of a better job and more money.

I hope I shan't be misunderstood. I believe in vocational education, and believe our country needs more and better opportunities than it is now enjoying. But, important as it is, it is only a

19

part of our whole educational program and its rapid development has overshadowed and has even tended to stifle the educational opportunities which prepare one for living rather than for gaining a livelihood. If our friendly critics from other lands and other types of civilization are right (and whether they are right or wrong, they are at any rate unanimous), we as a people are very much better hands at earning a living than we are at living — assuming that privilege to be more or less fully earned.

Perhaps I should point out at this place one apparent exception to the overwhelming predominance of the vocational in adult education. To describe it, I shall have to coin a phrase. Let me call it " pointed education." Teaching of this type hasn't to do with earning a living, nor need it be self-supporting. Offhand, one might be tempted to regard it as liberal education. But in all its multifarious manifestations, pointed education always presents this characteristic. In every case, somebody is willing to pay in order that other people may think as he does. These projects are at bottom really missionary rather than educational. We may accept the sincerity of those who support enterprises of this character, as we find them in the field of social hygiene, for example, or in " Americanization " and citizenship, or workers' education. We may admit the good quality of much of the work of this type, but because of its limitation, none of these activities touches the real nub of the question we are now discussing. As Heywood Broun has said in one of his lay sermons, " Education is nothing if it gives a man anything less than an opportunity to choose for himself the things which he will believe." If pointed education were real education, we could learn more from Soviet Russia just now than from any other country, for Moscow is conducting a nation-wide campaign in the teaching of adults.

This doesn't mean that adult education should avoid subjects on which people disagree. I cannot quote from any representative American document in this matter, because we have not as yet nationally recognized the importance of education for adults. We have before us, however, the report of an Adult Education Committee which the British government thought it worth while to set up in the dark days of 1916, and in this report we find the following significant sentences: " In the realm of adult education, controversial studies cannot be ruled out, for their exclusion would cut the heart out of the social impulse which has been so largely responsible for the growing demand for adult education. . . . The basis of discrimination between education and propaganda is not the particular opinions held by the teachers or the students, but the intellectual competence and quality of the former and the seriousness and continuity of study of the latter."

What nationally we lack the most, as I see it, is the habit — and in most communities the opportunity as well — of consecutive study in some subject for its own sake — history, literature, science, the fine arts, what you will — not to fill the pay envelope, directly or indirectly, but to develop in the student what experience has proved to be one of the most durable satisfactions of human life. The study must be *consecutive*, for the scattered lectures upon this and upon that, on which we have been relying since the days of the old lyceum, stimulating as they may be for the moment, leave no permanent impression. They don't really educate.

This overwhelming emphasis on the vocational in our adult education isn't inevitable. In England and in Denmark, for example, the two countries which have most to teach us, the most interesting work is being done in the non-vocational field. In England any group of men or women willing to give up one evening a week for three

years and to pay a very small fee from their own
pockets, can, through the good offices of the Workers' Education Association, obtain first, a grant in
aid from the British government, second, a supply
of books from the Carnegie United Kingdom
Trust, third, a competent teacher from Oxford or
Cambridge or one of the municipal universities.
These English classes are significant chiefly as a
demonstration of what can be done. The total
numbers involved are not very great, some 30,000
in all. We have before us, however, in the little
kingdom of Denmark, an example of how a system
of non-vocational adult education can literally
change the spirit of a whole nation. After the war
of 1864 and the loss of Schleswig and Holstein,
Danish morale was at a dangerously low ebb.
Within two or three generations, however, the
national spirit has literally been made over, partly
through the adoption of the principle of co-operation in agriculture and marketing, but primarily
through a system of folk schools which the people
themselves built up. It is estimated that to-day
almost one-third of the young people of the agri-
cultural population are voluntarily attending these
schools. The courses are short — five months in
winter for the boys, and three in summer for the
girls; they are strictly non-vocational in character

— Denmark provides other schools, also well-attended, in agriculture and other vocations. These folk schools are run on the simplest lines, and the whole investment involves a cost too small for us spendthrift Americans even to imagine.

It is very unlikely that any system — English, Danish, or any other — can be transported bodily to meet our needs here. It seems much more probable that our main line of development in cultural education for adults will be to broaden our existing programs in the vocational field. We need, however, to undertake as promptly as possible a sympathetic study of the efforts in non-vocational education now scattered and unrelated, which have sprung up all over the country. One of the investigators of the Carnegie Corporation reported that by all odds the most effective teaching of adults which he saw anywhere was in a class of working girls conducted last summer at Bryn Mawr. I believe that from such an examination might be drawn lessons of nation-wide importance. The very number and variety of these projects, and the fact that they have most of them grown up spontaneously, is a most encouraging sign of the time.

Some of these, like the Williamstown Conference, are well known but are not usually thought of as agencies for adult education. Others are almost unknown — a mountain school here and there in the South, an adaptation of the Danish folk school in Pennsylvania, a workers' group in Arkansas, a course for foremen in an industrial town, a study group of executives in a great corporation, and the reading and discussion groups, such as Amherst recently set out to develop among her alumni. Perhaps the best work in project education to-day is being done with the enlisted men in the army.

I venture to predict that in much we are now doing, we shall have to turn back from our present practices and start afresh. When, for example, we look at the actual technique of teaching cultural subjects to adults, we find a beautiful example of the lack of proper contact between our educational leadership and our adult education. Of course, one can point to many examples of excellent teaching, but they are not typical, and, in most cases, they are accidental. The usual process is to cut off cold slices of university courses, add water and perhaps a little sugar, and serve.

And yet the whole field is extraordinarily interesting and stimulating from the teacher's point of view. The students are going forward on their own steam instead of being gently impelled by parental or social pressure along the well-oiled grooves of "regular" education. Perhaps the situation which a teacher of a class of working-men must face can best be described by including a paragraph or two from a staff report which has recently come under my eye:

Working-men must first be interested and only then instructed. Economic law and historic fact must be made palatable without tampering with ingredients. A new type of teacher and a new idiom must be worked out, for adults cannot be taught as adolescents are. They have already done a day's work. They come with some experience in life. They require a body of material closely related to their immediate problems, whether personal or occupational. No class is academically homogeneous. The best work is now being done by college teachers, men liberal by belief, somewhat rebellious against the tediousness of teaching uninterested college youths, and appreciative that they can learn as much by contact with men who come with experience, as the men can learn from them.

While Gown has slumbered and slept so far as cultural education for adults is concerned, other agencies have been more alert. As has already been pointed out, in the large cities, the museums of art and science have developed educational activities of great interest. Perhaps most significant of all, the American public library, the country over, has made for itself a place in education which is unique in the history of the world. But the reading and study programs of the libraries, useful as they are, necessarily miss one great element in any scheme of education, and that is the element of discussion. Some way must be found to fit the library's contribution into the other parts of the educational offering.

Another matter to which our wise men must address themselves is to find some way whereby the extra-mural student who has demonstrated outstanding ability may, if he desires, be transferred to the university or to whatever environment may be the best for his fullest development, with no questions asked as to fees or entrance credits or certificates. I am not referring to the student who is merely competent or merely industrious, but to the man or woman who has shown the possibility of becoming distinguished. In any environment or under any conditions, there are only a few who can be recognized as of really superior quality, but these few should be discovered and given the keys of the city.

Perhaps the present generation does not know why the college and university of to-day seem so timid about taking a chance with the candidate who does not wear the formal wedding garment of $15\frac{1}{2}$ duly authenticated entrance units, or whatever the total at the moment may be. It is because in the late 'nineties and early nineteen hundreds, a husky young coal-heaver or longshoreman who had announced an earnest purpose to overcome the deficiencies of early education, could easily obtain admission as a special student at the rival college or university (never at one's own) — such aspirant appearing a week or so later in the line of the enemy football team. In the attempt to check these athletic abuses and to conform to the requirements of various standardizing agencies, the special student, who has or ought to have a very real place in our scheme of things, has practically disappeared.

There is no reason why the colleges, in their own interest, should not become much more generous than they now are, particularly with the present available tests of natural aptitude and the greater personal attention now given to questions of admission and supervision. From the point of view of adult education as a whole, such freedom, even though it might be exercised in only a few cases, would, I am sure, have an extraordinarily stimulating effect.

This question of tests of aptitude brings me to another point. So far as I know, the whole movement, both vocational and non-vocational, is going forward without the benefit of what we are just beginning to understand about educational measurements of capacity and accomplishment, although these measurements, particularly those of capacity, are obviously more important in extramural education than within the four walls of the college class.

Not so long ago, when numbers were small, the question whether a given student was capable of profiting fully by such extra-mural courses as he might desire to take was relatively unimportant except to himself; and, as a matter of fact, he was pretty sure to profit, because, without his knowing it, he was the product of a process of selection. Even if he were not intellectually gifted, he had at least shown courage and initiative enough to swim against the current.

To-day, however, the whole picture has changed. Students in adult education of various kinds have increased in number, not arithmetically but geometrically. The element of imitativeness, of which we all know the power, is in full operation.

Young people are now subject to a terrific "selling" pressure. There are at least five thousand highly paid and highly skilled correspondence-school salesmen at work all the time. One can hardly open a magazine without being faced either by an inspirational article in the reading matter or by an illustrated advertisement showing, for example, a young man who has taken somebody's correspondence course and is therefore sitting at the president's desk, from which he looks down with proud pity upon the shabby and cringing contemporary who failed to profit by his correspondence opportunities. In a word, we can no longer assume that men and women will enter adult education as a result of superior energy and power of deliberate decision any more than we can assume the students in our colleges to be impelled by the motive of intellectual interest. It is reported that nineteen out of twenty of the registrants in correspondence courses drop out before the completion of the course, and the mortality in all forms of extra-mural education is far higher than in regular courses, though the latter is high enough, in all conscience. Under the conditions necessarily controlling adult education, we must expect in any case a relatively high mortality, but is there anything we can do to keep it within

bounds? For one thing, a way must be found to
enable students to distinguish between *bona fide*
correspondence schools and those which are simply
swindles. It is a fact that anyone " who has published an article " can become a candidate for the
Ph.D. degree in an institution legally empowered
to grant that degree, the institution offering more
than eight hundred courses, conducted by a faculty
consisting of a man and his wife, both of them
government clerks, aided by their only child.

The most important way, however, to prevent
the present wastage is to provide an adequate sift-
ing device. It may be too much to expect institutions run on strict business principles, as practically all of them are, to turn away customers by a
rigid system of admission requirements, but why
should not the student himself take the initiative?
Why should he not arrange for his own entrance
test? He would do so, I am sure, if he realized just
how much of an investment of money, time, and
energy a serious course involves, and if he under-
stood the almost uncanny accuracy of the prog-
nosis provided by the best types of educational
measurements. The machinery for tests of this
character already exists. Some forty thousand
college students are tested annually, and with very
slight modifications, the questions could be made

available for the adult-education student. The suggestion may prove a little shocking to our present conventions, but, after all, there should be no more hesitation about being tested for one's capacity to profit by a course of instruction organized for a given level of maturity (and that is all the so-called intelligence test really amounts to) than about having one's eyes examined by an oculist. A test, or rather a series of them, is particularly important in the case of those who have left school early for any reason other than actual financial necessity. Human nature isn't so stupid, after all; and if a healthy boy or girl finds school work a bore, it means, in most cases, simply that the particular type of artificial experience which we call class instruction is not likely to be profitable for that particular person. A suitable test might bring out real capacity for learning certain manual skills in the case of a person for whom further book learning would be a waste of time.

Perhaps some of my readers have been thinking that this is all a highly theoretical and probably impracticable discussion, one which we call, and which we debase the word by calling, an "academic" discussion. Don't things of this kind work themselves out, on the whole, pretty well? If these hypothetical questioners are right, and if we can afford to let things work themselves out, it will simplify things tremendously. We can, for example, placidly watch the rapid increase in the hours of leisure for manual workers, coupled as this increase usually is with a decrease in the variety and interest of the work itself, and have no concern with making increased provision for the profitable improvement of these added hours in which the individual is free to choose what he shall do. Mechanical appliances and prepared foods, it may be said in passing, are rapidly creating the same leisure-time problem for the housewife. We need not agree with George W. Alger that " a civilization that bores its beneficiaries is perhaps even worse than one which overworks its slaves." When we read that in New York City alone there are each year at least twice as many homicides as in England and Wales, we can ignore the implication of the immensity of the group of the unadjusted and unhappy from which the participants in our appalling crime record must be drawn. We are free to assume that it does no particular harm for millions of well-meaning people to be stampeded in this wild direction or in that, all for the lack of any knowledge or conception of truths they might readily have learned from man's previous experience. We need have no concern over the general state of mental and cultural activity in our community, with our proportion of Babbitts and, by the same token, with the proportion of gifted men who go through life handicapped by the crudities and limitations of an Arrowsmith. If there is no connection between these matters and adult education, the discussion *is* theoretical. It is, in the bad sense of the word, " academic." If, on the other hand, we are not satisfied with things as they are, and if we are not fatalists, it is, I submit, well worth while to turn our attention to adult education, not as a means of bringing about the millennium, but as an agency of very definite importance in making life better worth living for the American citizen.

ADULT EDUCATION, TODAY AND TOMORROW [1]

IF THIS were the year of Grace, 1923, or even 1924, and if one of you had wanted to know how many men and women in the United States were supplementing their major job in life, whatever that might be — profession, business, trade, home-making — by using their minds seriously and consecutively (I don't mean an occasional lecture or an occasional solid book); if you had asked this, I could not have made the wildest guess. Today I can tell you that there must be well over three million. If the question had been as to what and where and how these people were carrying on their studies, I should have been equally at sea, for at that time neither I nor anyone else knew the answer. No one knows it fully today, but at least a good start has been made in getting at the facts.

I am not going to take your time now to go into the details of the many different types of adult

[1] Recognition Day, Chautauqua Institution, August 18, 1926, Chautauqua, N. Y.

35

education, for these are available in print, or soon will be. I shall try rather to consider the problems that are common to all these types; to tell what is being done to solve some of these, and to outline what, in my opinion, still remains to be done before adult education in America can be said to be on a sound basis.

We are beginning to realize all along the line that education as a secondary activity has very different qualities from education as a primary activity. There is the element of fatigue to consider for example, the unevenness of preparation; on the other hand, there is usually a background of practical experience that is lacking in the case of the so-called regular student, who as a matter of fact may really be very far from regular, but that is beside our present point. The teacher of adults can also count on the fact that his pupil is studying of his own volition, presumably at some sacrifice of time and energy, and is not acting merely under external compulsion, parental or social.

We are beginning to appreciate the problems involved in the technique of instructing such people; the need of specially trained and perhaps specially minded teachers, and of new teaching material for them, and the need also of special facilities to permit those who so wish to work without a teacher.

ADULT EDUCATION, TODAY AND TOMORROW

Two years ago, if a foreigner of inquiring mind had come to our shores in search of information and suggestions about the education of adults, a Dane, for example, for in Denmark, adult education is taken very seriously indeed, he would have had to pick up such information as he might here and there, and more or less at random. Today he would find an American National Association for Adult Education, both ready and able to help him, and he would find as its President a man with an almost uncanny instinct for concerning himself with the education of tomorrow rather than that of yesterday, or even of today. It is a good augury for adult education that Dean Russell of Teachers College has been willing to take this responsibility of leadership. The Board of Directors includes leaders in the Chautauqua and forum movements, of the public educational systems, of university extension, of the libraries, of labor classes, mountain schools, and shop schools.

Now this Association stands ready to do more than to satisfy the curiosity of the individual, be he foreigner or citizen. It will gather together and distribute accurate information to its members, both as to American and Foreign developments. It will make itself responsible for advice regarding needed researches and demonstrations.

I think however its greatest usefulness will prove to be as a source of advice to communities as to how they may organize and co-ordinate what they already have, and how, if necessary, they may supplement it in order that the citizen of that community may have available a well-balanced educational ration.

We have gone far enough to realize that it is the community which is the real unit with which we have to deal, and not the type of study in which the individual may be interested. Instead of discussion as to the abstract merits of vocational studies *vs.* cultural, and expressions of distress that we haven't more of the latter, what we really need are some good local demonstrations of this balanced ration, and how the inhabitants thrive on it.

Let me give another reason for the importance of this community integration. The element of discussion is where thus far we have fallen short most conspicuously. Our students are lectured to, or more likely, they read to themselves and write to their teachers. Without some local co-ordination, therefore, some planning and leadership, the individual students can't possibly get the play of mind upon mind which has proved to be the crowning merit of the English workers' education classes.

Not only has this new American Association come into being within the past few months, but there is evidence on every hand of a new recognition of the importance of adult education. The American Library Association has a vigorous department. The Bureau of Education at Washington has now a regularly appointed Specialist in Adult Education. An informal group of representatives of a few of the stronger proprietary correspondence schools has been formed, known as the Home Study Conference, in the interest of higher educational standards. This seems to be of particular significance, because it is these correspondence schools, much more than the older educational agencies, which have demonstrated what we may call the adult education market in this country, by which I mean the hundreds of thousands of people who are willing to invest in the cause of further education, not only their leisure time and their energy but a very substantial share of their money. The latest figures available show that these schools collect at least $75,000,000 annually in fees.

Not only will these agencies be in a position to gather and distribute information to those specially interested, but the general public will not be overlooked. This fall the Macmillan Company

will inaugurate a series of volumes on adult education by publishing the results of some of the
studies which have been made under the initiative
of the Carnegie Corporation. These will include
" The Young Worker " by Owen Evans, " University Extension " by Hall-Quest, " The Correspondence School and the Lyceum " by Noffsinger,
" New Schools for Older Students " by Nathaniel
Peffer, and " The Library and Adult Education"
by a commission of the American Library Association.

Dorothy Canfield is at work on a series of articles
for McCall's Magazine, which will later be published in book form by Harcourt, Brace and Company.

Today the implications that education is essentially a continuing process and that after maturity
it needn't be haphazard are to be found on every
hand. It is being realized that ways must be found
to " combine the new knowledge with the new
leisure."

I was much interested recently in coming upon
a definition of education by John Dewey, " the
enterprise of supplying the conditions which in-
sure growth, or adequacy of life, *irrespective of
age*." I was interested also in noting that when
the farm women were asked not long ago what

they wanted out of life to make them happy, they placed opportunity for further education high on their list. A very practical man, though a far-seeing one, — for there is no necessary contradiction, — is Owen D. Young, and I give great weight to his statement, made not long ago, that American industry must for the future be based not on a living wage alone, nor on a saving wage, but on a cultural wage.

Another significant thing is the way in which the educational aspects of great national movements are becoming more clearly recognized. Success in public health and other social work doesn't depend on telling people how to live and what to do or to leave undone, but on teaching them — and there's a deal of difference between telling and teaching. Politics is recognizing the same thing and so is organized business. In none of these fields have we fully succeeded in making the distinction between education and propaganda, but that will come with time. The co-operation of parent and teacher in the interest of young children is also turning out to be a process of educating the parent, even the father.

Not only the libraries, as we have seen, but the museums are beginning to recognize that their job is essentially an educational one. John Cotton

41

Dana, who is one of the major prophets of this generation, is conducting a museum in the city of Newark, which shows how far the new conception has gone and which will repay the study of anyone interested in this field.

By the way, don't let me leave the impression that I think all that is new in adult education is good nor that all that is good is new. Chautauqua for example is not new — as conscious adult education goes in America, it is very old — and yet you are here to say that it is good, and I am here to agree with you.

Adult education, old and new, is very much in the air today. There is a great deal of it going on and very many people are affected, but don't think that it is all over but the shouting. Quite the contrary, there is some danger that the shouting is taking place in advance of any real justification for it. The situation as I see it is this. We have the best opportunities in the world's history for furthering the education of adults, abundance of leisure time, an economic leeway, the like of which has never been seen, a very high degree of literacy and a national belief in education and what it can do, which is almost naïve in its trustfulness. We have furthermore in the specific business of conducting adult education a very vigorous going concern, or rather a number of very different and largely unrelated going concerns, dealing in the aggregate with a very large and rapidly growing number of individuals.

Outstanding examples of these are to be found in the extension services of state universities, — Wisconsin, for example, or California, — the rapidly growing interest of endowed universities like Columbia, in the public night schools in the more progressive cities, in the best of the correspondence schools, in the class work of national organizations like the Y. W. C. A.; of libraries like Cleveland and Indianapolis; of labor groups in Milwaukee and Cincinnati; of museums like the one in Newark already mentioned, and the great institutions of New York and Chicago. Immense educational enterprises are carried on by the United States government, notably in its two newest departments, Agriculture and Commerce. We have also scattered through the country a number of local experiments, all of them modest, but some of them of significance as destined to point the way for future progress.

All this is to the good, but it isn't enough. Instead of glowing with pride that so many do find ways to go on with their education, we should blush to think that so many fail to do so. I could give you a long catalogue of things that need to be done before our adult education is really on a sound basis, but they are all or very nearly all manifestations, more or less direct, of lack of adjustment between this type of education and education in general, a lack of appreciation that it isn't something separate but is an essential part of a larger whole.

I have a friend, a railway official, who recently set out to give me some adult education. Among other things he informed me that when the Twentieth Century is running at her normal speed and on a level track, the strain on the tie-bars is only twenty pounds, also that on the average it costs about fifty dollars to stop a train. In telling me this my friend unwittingly furnished me with a text for my sermon today. What he really means of course is not that it cost fifty dollars to stop the train, but to start it up again. Now a train isn't the only thing that costs something to start up, if once you have let it stop. When we describe adult education as it is conducted today we are in effect talking about this expensive process of starting up a train which has been permitted to stop. Why need it have stopped? People don't cease to eat at some particular point in their lives, with commencement exercises to mark the event, and then perhaps years after, have to be cajoled, besought and inspired to resume the habit. It is no exaggeration to say that adult education in a vast majority of cases is sold today rather than bought and this I believe is because the appetite for learning has been lost.

The continuation schools which we borrowed from Germany and which we started a few years ago with a flourish of trumpets, have in general not been a success, and although there are a number of factors which might account for this failure, the inability of the common schools to instill a desire for more is I think the most important.

Why should we treat the nourishment of our stomachs in one way and that of our minds in another? Some people acquire the appetite for feeding their minds and retain it through life, people who, almost literally, would starve if they could not get this nourishment. These are normal people. Why aren't there more of them? Isn't it fair to ask this question of the agencies of formal education? Have they given the students under their direction an impression of education as a continuing process? Have they done all that they could to develop a permanent appetite for it? I don't hesitate to say that formal education neither recognizes the importance of this element of continuity nor is doing what it might to prepare the minds of students to carry it out in their own lives.

Of course good teaching stimulates curiosity and the person who retains his curiosity comes to recognize what John Erskine calls the moral obligation to be intelligent. Teaching of this kind, however, is all too rare in any branch of learning, and all too often the student drops any particular course of study with a sense of profound relief. There is no question in his case of getting up from the table hungry.

The importance of realizing this objective does not lessen as successive stages in our system of formal education are passed. Quite the contrary, the farther along we go the more highly selective is the group with which we are dealing and the greater the potential usefulness to the community. It is particularly important that college graduates should not lose intellectual momentum, and yet as the president of a college famous in our history has recently pointed out, college alumni as a body represent about as perfect an example of arrested development as is to be found in our population. When we remember the extraordinary devotion of the alumnus to his alma mater, it is amazing that only here and there is any effort made to guide this loyalty and devotion along intellectual lines.

46

Dr. Wickenden says, " A college that gives its graduates a finished education is a failure. Only that college succeeds which equips its graduates for a life-time of self-education. Let us hope that the day is not far off when commencement will not mark the end of one thing and the beginning of another, but a mile-stone in a long, long trail that runs to the end of life."

Nor need we stop at the college. A professional degree should furnish no immunity from further study, either technical or what is possibly more important, cultural.

Perhaps we shall have better results from the application of the newer educational ideas as they are being manifested under the Dalton Plan or in the Lincoln School, or the school library movement, or in the honors programs in colleges, or as they are just beginning to get a hearing in medicine and engineering and commerce. All these are encouraging, for they aim at initiative on the part of the student rather than passive receptivity, but as yet they haven't even touched the great mass.

The inculcation of curiosity, the hunger for more, is the great need, but it's a long job, for it will require not only a radically different attitude of mind on the part of most teachers, but infinite patience, a steadfast refusal to be discouraged and a recognition that under the best conditions the score will be far from perfect. There is, however, a secondary need, much more practical and much more easy to meet. The student, when he goes to work, as we say, should possess not only the desire to carry on his education but also some definite information as to just how he can do it.

The situation as I see it may be described as follows: Each individual goes a certain distance, shorter or longer, along a series of clearly marked roads, kindergarten, elementary and secondary school, college, technical school, university. Sooner or later he leaves the road and strikes out for himself in open country. Now in this open country there are paths or roads (the various agencies of adult education) upon which he may continue his journey. Some of them are in excellent repair, but with rare exceptions they never join the highway, and consequently the traveler must spend precious time and lose even more precious momentum in wandering aimlessly before he continues his journey at the speed of which he is capable. The great majority never find any of these paths at all and such progress as they make is halting and unsatisfactory.

And all this is true largely because the main

highway is lacking in sign posts, giving information as to the paths of continuing education. It is known that only a handful of those who start on these highways can continue very far, and for everyone they come to an end earlier or later. It is also known when the travelers leave the road in greatest numbers, beginning with the day when working papers may be taken out, then at the end of the junior or senior high school or junior or senior college course, and so on. These are the points where sign posts are obviously the most needed and where they are conspicuous by their absence.

All of which is a fanciful way of saying that education as a primary occupation does little or nothing to prepare the student for continuing his education as a secondary occupation. The studies which have been carried on under the direction of the Carnegie Corporation have made abundantly clear that there is almost universally a lag between leaving school and taking up adult education. This lag in the case of the typical university extension student must be at least eight years, and it is equally long in the case of the correspondence student. For the student in night school, public or private, it is four or five years.

I submit that there is no more important objective for formal education than to prepare the student's mind for the need and practicability of continuing the process. Without this we shall never know what adult education might achieve did it not have to use so much of its energy in the unnecessary process of re-starting the train.

As much as anything else we need a demonstration of what intelligent co-operation between the regular teacher and the extra-mural agencies might accomplish. Practically all that we have today is the not yet satisfactory experiment of the continuation schools, and a study, made in Indianapolis, published by the A. L. A. under the title "Older Boys and Girls Out of School." In this study the librarian and not the teacher took the initiative. An experiment ought to be tried on a large scale and possibly over a term of years with the full modern technique of personnel work and follow-up, educational measurement and the rest. I have hope that the American Association for Adult Education may find itself able to take up and carry through such a study, or rather a series of studies, for those leaving the grades, the high school, the college and the university.

It is of great significance that the painstaking scientific studies which characterize the progress of education during the past twenty-five years are really beginning to carry over into this field. As one result we are about ready to say with assurance of scientific confirmation that adults are really able to learn at all. I mean, of course, to the degree that a course of study is a good investment. Obviously our brain as a machine changes its manner of functioning as the years pass. Children, for example, can learn languages practically without effort and much more rapidly and successfully than older people do at great effort. The general scientific opinion, so far as science has had any opinion on the subject, has been that all along the line the capacity to learn new things falls very rapidly after the early twenties. And it is characteristic of the divorce between educational science and adult education that this seemed to worry nobody during the rapid growth of an enterprise which now costs the participants directly or indirectly fully $100,000,000 a year. The most recent studies, as I have indicated, look to a much longer term of fruitful learning.

The need of a general study of the psychology of reading has just been pointed out by the American Library Association. We know a good deal about how children learn to read but very little about how or what or why adults read. And yet Mr. Carnegie alone contributed more than $50,000,000

51

toward making it possible and comfortable for them to do so.

Next fall will witness the first co-ordinated experiment for the preparation of teachers of adults and the study of class progress. In this, for the first time, so far as I know, there will be applied to the problems and practices of adult education what we have learned in general education as to the measurements of capacity and achievement both of teacher and class.

Outside of a classroom we give our adult student no chance to have the satisfaction of measuring by tests in whose reliability he himself has confidence what he has accomplished, in terms of what others have achieved. Why, for example, should not the A. L. A. set up a series of tests, not the old-fashioned examination, but the modern scientific product, to measure the reader's mastery of the different courses in its admirable series of " Reading with a Purpose " and have these given in the public libraries throughout the country?

While our general need as I see it is to establish a more logical relation between adult education and formal education there are also other things which we need to think through. For example, there is the relation between adult education and recreation. If any of you have ever happened to travel abroad with a conscientious German tourist you will remember the great contrast between his preparation for the trip and your own. Here at home the museums which are now being established in our national parks are an interesting and significant step toward the enrichment of the experience of those who visit these Parks.

Then there is the question of the Fine Arts. We have the best opportunities in the world to hear music. More important architectural monuments are being erected here today than perhaps in all other countries combined. We are rapidly becoming the custodians, public and private, of much of the world's treasure in painting and sculpture. And yet it is only beginning to occur to us that one way for us as a people to get the solace and the delight which comes from an appreciation of beauty is to learn something about the different arts. I don't mean strings of names and dates to be memorized, but something very different. Here is a wonderful opportunity for an adult education that is re-creative. The current interest in the non-commercial drama touches alike recreation, the arts, and adult education, and is one of the most encouraging signs of the times. The British government, by the way, has recently published a most interesting and informing report on " The Drama and Adult Education," which may be purchased from His Majesty's Stationery Office for the sum of one shilling.

Let me sum up in closing. We know that the training of adults is not a minor but a major educational activity. We are beginning to realize on the one hand the extraordinary possibilities of its development, and on the other its special needs and problems. We have the organized leadership to meet these, both in furthering research and demonstration and in community integration. We are feeling our way toward better co-ordination with other activities, notably recreation and the arts. Finally, and in my judgment, most important, we must see to it that learning is a continuing process not only in theory but more and more in fact; that we now suffer a loss of momentum that is as costly as it is unnecessary, and that to remedy this our chief job is after all to educate the educators.

PLAYBOYS OF THE COLLEGE
WORLD [1]

To ONE who spent many years in rather close
contact with American colleges and American undergraduates, and who has now returned to these
contacts after a lapse of seven years, the outstanding change between that day and this is the greatly
increased interest on the part of the students in all
matters which have to do with the arts. Although
the advance in collegiate music is impressive, the
situation is even more striking with reference to
the drama.

The march has been so rapid that if I were to
describe things as they were in the old days, say
fifteen years ago, the average undergraduate of
to-day would hardly believe it. I don't mean that
there was no acting; of course there was, and some
of it very good, but the typical play was fourth-
rate rubbish, the stage accessories and the lighting
were of the crudest, and no one seemed to mind.
The actors knew no better, and it made no difference to the handful of their fellow students who

[1] An article first published in *Scribner's Magazine*, January,
1926, and reprinted by courtesy of that publication.

formed the " house." Altogether, dramatics was a
very minor sport indeed. To-day, in almost every
college, from Portland to Portland, dramatics is
distinctly a major sport. The students have the
highest standards as to the literary and dramatic
value of the plays they present, and their interest
is not confined to acting itself, but includes writing
for the stage and the direction of performances and
goes deeply into questions of stage setting, lighting, and costuming. Indeed, it is the only undergraduate activity which can compete with athletics. The dramatic clubs are usually limited in
numbers, with long waiting lists; but the student
body at large is interested, and items of stage lore
are taking their place with athletic dope in undergraduate conversation.

Just what has happened to bring about this
change? For the past three or four years the drama
has been epidemic and no one can say how a new
victim catches the fever. But if we go back to the
comparatively recent past of, say, six years ago, we
can nearly always trace the infection in any particular college to some enthusiastic junior in the
department of English, usually one who had come
under the influence of George Baker at Harvard,
and who either woke up a dormant dramatic so-
ciety or, more likely, built up a new one out of his

own classes, or hers. Though the innovator's interest was normally in plays and acting, there is an interesting case where an enthusiast for the establishment of a standard English speech was the initiator of a strong acting tradition in a State university. These pioneers had to combat faculty inertia, on the one hand, and the student fear of being thought highbrow, on the other. But they had the real apostolic spirit, and they succeeded beyond all expectations.

This advance in college dramatics has been intertwined with the nation-wide Little Theatre movement. The undergraduate movement is by no means a mere offshoot of the other; on the whole, the influence runs rather the other way, particularly if one includes as college work such professional opportunities as Professor Baker offered at Harvard and Mr. Stevens and his associates have given at the Carnegie Institute of Technology. The direction of the non-academic Little Theatres is largely in the hands of college men and women — eleven Oberlin graduates, for example, hold such positions — and the players and audiences are drawn largely from college alumni.

Although the stage tradition is oldest in the men's colleges and the women's, these have been outstripped by the co-educational institutions, which we provincials on the Atlantic seaboard are prone to forget outnumber the separate institutions by 332 to 199, more than a third of the latter being Roman Catholic colleges. In other words, it is in the State and municipal universities and in the evangelical colleges which have grown up throughout the Middle West during the last century that college dramatics has taken the strongest hold. Most of their students come to these freshwater institutions without ever having seen anything in the spoken drama better than their own high school play. Nevertheless, an astonishing number of them turn out to be excellent material. I am told that the first thing to be done is to eradicate almost wholly what they conceive to be acting, from their memories of the moving picture theatres. They all overact, because they have no realization of the differences between the necessities of the spoken and of the unspoken drama. In spite of all this, those who have taught on both sides of the Alleghanies say that there is a certain freshness and enthusiasm in the Middle Western youngster which more than counterbalances the greater sophistication of the Easterner. In the rapid spread of its influence, the stage seems to have broken down pretty thoroughly all the barriers of denominational and other restrictions. In the very colleges which used to avoid the immorality of the stage by teaching Shakespeare as literature (though they didn't try to teach music by a silent reading of the score), wings have now sprouted from the chapel platform. Perhaps there has been no such partnership between the church and stage since the Middle Ages.

Not so long ago, nothing was more local in its influence than a college play. To-day the performances at Iowa City and Berkeley, at Cornell and at Chapel Hill, and a score of other places, are news in New York. Hillsdale College, in Michigan, and Ottawa University, in Kansas, can hardly be included among our more prominent institutions of learning; yet what they do in the drama is duly recorded in the serious theatre magazines. If you turn over the advertising pages of *The Theatre Arts Magazine,* you can learn that Stanford and Iowa and Northwestern are paying cash to tell you about their courses in the drama.

What do the students play? Perhaps the best way to answer the question is to record a few of the last year's actual offerings. The Cornell Dramatic Club, for example, put on thirty-two plays, usually giving two and three performances of each, and including the first performance in English, of a comedy by Cervantes, a mediæval farce, the third performance, in English, of a Jacques Copeau play, and examples of Sudermann, Anatole France, Drinkwater, and, nearer home, Booth Tarkington and Eugene O'Neill.

At Grinnell College, in Iowa, last year's bill included, in addition to notable one-acts by Synge, Lady Gregory, and Lewis Beach, "Romeo and Juliet," Shaw's "Arms and the Man," Rostand's "Les Romanesques," Barry's "You and I," Michael Arlen's "Ace of Thirteens," Henry Arthur Jones's "The Goal," and an original All College Revue.

At Iowa, a dozen long plays are staged, together with a number of one-act plays. Here is the list of the former: Flavin's "Children of the Moon," Barrie's "Alice-Sit-by-the-Fire," Shaw's "The Devil's Disciple," Mowatt's "Fasl.ion," Kaufman and Connelly's "Beggar on Horseback," Galsworthy's "The Silver Box," Shakespeare's "A Midsummer Night's Dream," Jesse Lynch Williams's "Why Not?" Carel Kapek's "R-U-R," Lewis Beach's "The Goose Hangs High," Euripides' "Iphigenia in Tauris," Dekker's "The Shoemaker's Holiday."

In their six years' career, the Penn State Players have presented twenty-nine long plays and ninety-seven one-act plays; a normal school in Missouri has put on six different plays by Shakespeare in as many years.

By increasing somewhat the list of colleges, we can add Sophocles to Euripides, Marlowe and Beaumont and Fletcher, Molière and Lope de Vega, to Shakespeare. From the stage of the eighteenth century we can add Schiller and Sheridan, and from the modern London stage, Pinero, Milne, Synge, and Dunsany. From the continental, Ibsen, Tchekov and Andreyev, Brieux, Molnar and Pirandello — " and a great many more of lesser degree, in sooth a goodly company." I won't retail the American playwrights, but I can testify that the students prefer the works of men and women that deserve and receive success on the professional stage to the offerings of the " literary " theatre.

A most interesting and significant element in the whole movement is what has already become the tradition in certain institutions, namely, to encourage original plays written by students and with local settings. These " folk plays," as they are usually called, include not only one-act pieces but full-size dramas. The University of North Dakota gives plays of this character, dealing with pioneer life, in its open air theatre, formed by an ox-bow in the small river that runs through Grand Forks. Since their professor of dramatics, Frederick Koch, migrated from North Dakota to North Carolina, the university at Chapel Hill has put on a number of plays, written and performed by students, and some of them of extraordinary merit, dealing with present-day mountain life or with local historical traditions. Georgia and South Carolina have followed their northern neighbor, and one of Professor Koch's pupils has carried the idea to the State University of Wyoming and thence to Arizona, thereby adding two new centres of local tradition, that of the Rockies and that of the Southwest border. The movement has been vital enough to impel two Chinese undergraduates in American colleges to write folk plays of their own land, and one of these has·been deemed worthy of publication in full in "The Golden Book." Sometimes the director takes a hand and adapts some ancient legend for the college stage — Mrs. Flanagan of Grinnell has recently put on two pantomimes of this character, one Egyptian and one Hindu.

It may be observed that the plays given by the college students for college audiences are as a whole distinctly not on what an Englishman would call the jolly side — perhaps because, as one of the college directors has pointed out, undergraduates are happy enough to love tragedy. On the other hand, the comic muse has a fair share of offerings, and the students and their teachers don't hesitate to turn from the classics to George Cohan, or to a home brew of what is perhaps the most characteristic dramatic form we have developed in America, our topical revue.

Oberlin was one of the first co-educational colleges to take up work in the drama, and its organization may be taken as typical. Dramatic activities are under the direction of one of the professors of English. The club is strictly limited in number to one hundred, and is divided into ten producing groups. A play is rehearsed by a group and is first performed before the club at large and criticised by the members. If it survives, it is given before the college, and finally goes farther afield — for the Oberlin actors, like many others, spend their Christmas and spring holidays on the road, their trips ranging from Chicago on the west to New York and Washington on the east. At Oberlin, as elsewhere, there is little or no outside help. The boys build the platform which enlarges the chapel stage. They look after the electrical work and plan and build the scenery, while the girls design and make the costumes. As an example of student co-operation in another college, the book and lyrics of a revue, in which the scenes are laid on the local campus, were written by the students of the English department; music was "adapted" by students in that department; physical education students put on the dances, and those in art designed and painted the scenery and co-operated with domestic science students in providing the costumes. As a result, fully a third of the student body took some active part in the production.

Next to its rapid growth, I have been most struck by the variety of the manifestations of this new student interest. It can't be pigeonholed as amateur, for Professor Baker's work at Harvard and his work to come at Yale are professional in spirit, as is that at Carnegie Tech. Furthermore, a college actor who takes up high school teaching to-day will find his stage experience to be a very definite vocational asset, because the interest in dramatics in the high schools is second only to that in the colleges. I am told, by the way, that the recent bachelors of arts who have become professional actors or playwrights far outnumber those who have devoted themselves to poetry or painting or music or any other of the arts, with the possible and understandable exception of architecture.

In a few places, stage work counts for a professional degree. In many others it may be offered toward the bachelor's degree, sometimes as a major; in still others the only reward is the fun of the game. Personally, I think these last are the most fortunate, though I fear the student wouldn't agree with me; because to do the thing for the fun of it is of the essence of the whole movement.

There is no blighting uniformity of eligibility rules. As Walter Prichard Eaton has pointed out, in the theatre your amateur standing isn't determined by whether you play summer baseball for money or sell golf clubs for John Wanamaker. The students living at International House, for example, who come from seventy-one countries and who attend forty-three different institutions in and about New York, have their dramatic organization and put on their own plays. Last year they gave a remarkable performance of Drinkwater's "Lincoln."

In the men's colleges the players are beginning to avoid the artificiality of masquerading the women's parts in serious modern plays by calling in faculty wives and daughters. The separate women's colleges haven't yet made the corresponding gesture, but perhaps they will before long. The semi-detached ones are working upon an exchange basis — Radcliffe with Harvard, for example. In the Washington Square Players, of New York University, and in other groups, no line is drawn between undergraduates and alumni. At Evanston, the local Little Theatre and the student club of Northwestern University are closely interrelated, and there is a similar situation at Columbia, South Carolina. Even the faculty is welcome, a department head at the University of Illinois having recently challenged the laurels of Cyril Maude by his performance of Grumpy.

After all, athletics and dramatics are branches of the same trunk. No human instinct is more deeply rooted than that for play, and this instinct, of which the first manifestations for young men and maidens was probably the dance, has from time immemorial tended to swing in one direction toward feats of physical prowess, and in another toward pageantry and the drama. Under the Puritan tradition which so deeply colored the early life of our colleges, physical sport did not happen to be specifically denounced as sin, and it came in time to be tolerated and then to grow into what we now find. The drama, on the other hand, though quite as normal an outgrowth of the play instinct, had to await a breakdown of the intolerances of the Puritan tradition. I don't mean that the breakdown is complete, there is plenty of evidence to the contrary, but within very recent years it has gone sufficiently far to give the drama its chance.

The fact that every sizable university and college has a stadium or is planning to erect one, points, whether we like it or no, to that permanence which comes with vested interests. The corresponding investment in facilities and equipment, though negligible as compared with that for athletics, is large enough to provide insurance, if insurance be needed, against our waking up some morning to find that college dramatics had disappeared overnight, like Mah-Jong or the crossword puzzle. I am not referring to the equipment for the professional study of the stage, such as that at the Carnegie schools, or that now being created at Yale, at the Chicago Art Institute, and at Rochester, where the Eastman School of Music has recently added dramatic action to its program. Nor have I in mind the great places of assembly like the Greek Theatre at Berkeley, for their use by the students is incidental. I am thinking, rather, of the rapidly increasing number of well appointed collegiate theatres, of which that at Dartmouth may be taken as typical of a building constructed for the purpose, and those at the University of Colorado and the University of

North Carolina as adaptations of older buildings. A new theatre is being erected at Brown for the Komians, and on the campus at Iowa the State is erecting a laboratory theatre admirably equipped, with an auditorium for six hundred people. In addition, the colleges are rapidly accumulating valuable collections of sets and other equipment, most of it home-made. That at Oberlin, for example, is valued at $10,000.

If, however, the development of dramatics has followed that of her elder sister in certain ways, it has broken sharply away in others. Thus far she has escaped the rigidity and conformity, I almost said the old-maidishness, of her senior. May she ever be free from it! In athletics, the country over, every one must do the same thing at the same time under the same rules, often without rhyme or reason. I have seen, for example, the University of Virginia playing football when it was too hot for the men to wear stockings. The college theatre, on the other hand, embraces all types — professional, vocational, with or without faculty or outsiders. The Californians take advantage of their climate and give outdoor pageants. The success of the folk plays depends, obviously, on devotion to the *genius loci.*

Even more striking is the difference in attitude

toward the world outside the college walls. In athletics, this world is counted on to fill the stadium and its youth to provide husky freshmen, and that is about all. The occasions are very rare where such interest as a college may take in the development of school or community sport cannot clearly be recognized as a recruiting move. Nothing could be more different than the situation in the drama. The students really want to help the work in the schools and to co-operate with that in the communities. They lend them props and other equipment with the greatest generosity. They give performances where there is not the slightest chance of meeting expenses. They don't hesitate to act in one-room schoolhouses lit by gasoline lamps. Here again, as might be expected, the missionary spirit is particularly strong in the institutions which emphasize the student folk play. The Carolina Playmakers, for example, show their plays in three States, having given performances last year in twenty-nine different schoolhouses and town halls. The hill towns have no theatres, but they furnish the most critical audience possible for this folk drama.

The partial rising of the cloud of intolerance and the nation-wide revival of interest which the drama shares with all the arts, plus the influence of a few inspiring leaders — these are enough to explain the new impulse in college dramatics. But are they enough to account for the extraordinary hit which the drama has made? May there have developed inside the life of the present-day college some elements which make its advent peculiarly welcome? I have consulted several of the play directors and teachers of the drama about this, but they weren't greatly interested. Being enthusiasts, they see no reason to seek for other causes than the virtues of the drama itself. I may, however, set forth four suggestions as to possible internal influences — confessing that I think most highly of the last two (which are my own).

Some one has made the interesting suggestion that the current cult for selling one's personality may have something to do with the boom in dramatics. Certainly, students to-day hear a great deal of the value of college life as a laboratory of social adjustments and a preparation for the mastery of one's fellow man — in a word, for " putting things over " — far more than they hear of the benefits which will accrue from what we used to call a sound education. And they may well be forgiven if they place too high an emphasis on these qualities, not only for profitable business careers, but for the advancement of education and politics and religion. How far a student who comes to college full of these ideas of salesmanship of self, or who picks them up after he arrives, deliberately selects the college stage to give him poise, to learn to stand or sit without fidgeting or sprawling, to accustom himself to the sound of his own voice if not of his own words, I don't know. I do remember an awkward and tongue-tied student of my own who told me later on that he had in cold blood forced his way into college dramatics for these reasons, and who, I may add, became a good actor and is now a good professor. On the other hand, the coaches of today question whether this is often a conscious influence on the part of the students who take up dramatics; one of them goes so far as to say it never is.

A reader of recent fiction dealing with the life of American undergraduates may well wonder whether the theatre has profited by the absorption of the students in questions dealing with the emotional relations between the sexes, which is set forth in such detail in these novels. How far the student turns to the stage as dealing with matters which he and his friends are constantly discussing, either for further enlightenment or as a sort of safety-valve, I leave for more competent persons to determine. Here again the teacher of dramatics is inclined to regard the factor as unimportant.

The first of my own theories is that, the whole movement being so young, teachers and coaches have not had time to lose their own enthusiasms and become cut-and-dried; and to this extent they have an advantage in the unrelenting contest for student patronage which goes on silently behind the façade in our republics of arts and sciences. These teachers of dramatics haven't lost faith in the doctrine that the normal youth really enjoys working with his head as well as with his legs, provided in each case he regards the work as worth while. The actual mental labor which many a student active in dramatics must undergo to learn three or even four major parts a year would, if he were willing to apply it to their courses, perhaps astonish as many professors who have lost, or perhaps never possessed, the art of tapping these sources of student energy.

Finally, I think that in more cases than either undergraduates or teachers recognize, the students who go in for dramatics are unconsciously seeking an escape from the trivialities of the complicated and highly artificial life they have built up for themselves. The war gave the men students a chance to break away from the conventionalized

pattern, but it was a chance from which they failed
to profit, and nowadays, when it is as much the
thing for the girls to go to college as for the boys,
with almost the same disregard for intellectual
qualifications, their community life is also becoming rapidly overloaded. In the days of youth real
living is imaginative living, and, somehow, these
young people have succeeded in building up for
themselves a singularly unimaginative existence.

A part in a good play must seem much more real
than the monotonous succession of the college
days. Such a day for a boy begins, let us say, by
skimming the college paper in chapel. Broken
somewhat by two or three classes and desultory
preparation therefor, and perhaps by some com-
pulsory exercise, it continues with a round of
chores for some " activity " or for the fraternity,
with watching other students perform and cheer-
ing them to order. Sometimes there will be a " pep
meeting " in addition. The evening's entertain-
ment will be a movie, a dance, or poker party.
Even worse than the banality of the life itself is
the interminable discussion as to its details that
goes on during meals and at other times.

The athletes are free while they are actually per-
forming, and the few who are real students have
a more permanent way of escape. But isn't many

a boy, of the great majority who are neither varsity material nor natural-born students, caught in this squirrel cage of trivialities, unconsciously bored with it all and groping for something to give a real fillip to existence, likely to find that for him "the play's the thing"? And isn't many a girl, for somewhat different but equally cogent reasons, likely to feel so too?

OPPORTUNITIES AND DANGERS
OF EDUCATIONAL
FOUNDATIONS [1]

YOUR committee on program must be gifted with prophetic vision. How otherwise could it have foreseen that since the time my associates and I were invited to contribute to this symposium, the right of these foundations to associate with universities at all would have been questioned, if not by the president and faculty, at any rate by the regents of one of the universities which compose this association. Whatever may be said as to the wisdom of the action of these regents, they have certainly added interest and piquancy to our discussion to-day.

The conventional view of the relation between the university and the foundation is that the university is the active and the foundation the passive element, the latter furnishing the paradox of an immortal body perpetually engaged in selling its life as dearly as possible.

[1] Paper presented at the New Haven meeting of the Association of American Universities, October 30, 1925.

75

While there is a certain element of truth in the conventional picture, it is significant that the proportion of foundation money which is going into grants for the general purposes of any college or university is steadily decreasing. In other words, foundation grants arc coming more and more to be in support of specific projects, and the initiative for these projects may come from anywhere — from an individual, from a foundation, from a university or perhaps most often from one of the national organizations of scholars.

The foundations are largely responsible for a new grouping, closely related to the universities in personnel and program, but usually independent of any single institution. Research in economics, for example, is to-day largely in the hands of such institutes, as they are usually called. In science, the National Research Council has itself become a foundation through a grant from the Carnegie Corporation.

Although the individual institution has therefore not so much to say as to the disposal of foundation funds as it had formerly, the contributions of the foundation to the university, if less direct, are more important than ever before. I don't think it an exaggeration to say that any important research project which has the endorsement of a

representative group of scholars can find financial
support from one or another of the foundations.
It is to be noted that the researches thus helped
cover a very wide range and include such practical
questions as the teaching of foreign languages and
the organization of professional schools of medicine or engineering.

Not only do all these enterprises give the ripe
scholar the chance to show his mettle, but recent
foundation activities are doing much to prepare
the scholars of the generation to come. I am told
that, in all, the foundations support nearly fifteen
hundred fellows annually, and of course at the
close of their incumbency the great majority either
return to or enter academic life.

In trying to make clear that the relations between university and foundation are far more
many-sided and complex than might appear offhand, I don't wish to minimize in any way the
debt of the foundation to the university. In all
seriousness, I don't see how the foundation could
carry out what I conceive to be its peculiar func-
tions without the university. The foundation may
be convenient, sometimes very convenient indeed
to the university, but the latter could get along
without it — it managed to do so for a good many
hundred years; the foundation, on the other hand,

is absolutely dependent on the university, or, to be more accurate, on university men and women.

In the first place, our executives and our expert staffs, when we have them, have been chiefly recruited from academic life, always from men of academic training and ideals. Our relations are with academic people, and we are constantly turning for advice to them, sometimes offhand and sometimes in a more formal manner. In the educational program of one of the foundations, for example, it is the practice of the trustees not to consider separate projects at all, but to limit their responsibility to the approval or disapproval of a year's schedule made up of specific enterprises, which, by a sort of preferential ballot, have been selected as most promising of important results by a committee of academic people. Another of the foundations gets its light upon matters of this kind by conducting what in the Catholic church would be called a " retreat." To formulate one branch of its program twenty-three of the leaders in this particular field, coming from thirteen institutions, were willing to devote ten days of their summer vacation; another group had a meeting of the same length, in which twelve men, representing ten institutions, did the same thing. In all three cases, the service of these advisers was wholly voluntary.

Most important of all, the university nearly always provides, directly or indirectly, the personnel to carry any project through, and helpful as the financial contribution to that end may be, it is always secondary in importance to the human contribution. This human contribution of the university is not limited to academic projects, but affects all the activities of the foundations. The American Law Institute, for example, was financed upon the recommendation of a group of judges and practicing lawyers. The actual restatement of each branch of the law (which is the task which the institute has undertaken) is being done by teams of university law professors. For a long time there was no close relation between the American public library and the American university, but to-day the librarians themselves have decided that what their profession most needs is the establishment of a university school of the highest type, and they have turned to a foundation to make this possible.

The university and the foundation are alike engaged in the same great enterprise, the advancement of human knowledge and understanding. Both work through human beings, and the job consists in choosing the right men and women, giving them the tools they need and then letting them alone. The common task is to find the individual and to set him to work, either singly or in teams (and co-operative research is perhaps the most significant contribution of our day).

In this task, the foundation supplements the university at its weakest points. It can provide freedom for immediate action. The fixed charges against its income are relatively insignificant as compared with those of the university, and it can usually put its hand on the funds needed. Apart from questions of money, furthermore, the smaller body steers more easily.

There are times when it is everything to be able to strike when the iron is hot. The assurance of an $8,000 grant to be distributed through the University of Toronto brought together three men, each with some special competence in dealing with the baffling problem of diabetes, men who otherwise could never have worked as a team, and these men developed insulin.

The foundation, also, from the nature of its contacts, can often get a more general view of needs and opportunities than seems possible for any single university. It inevitably becomes a sort of clearing house of academic ideas. Saving their presence, academic folk are as a group rather ignorant than otherwise of what their neighbors are doing and thinking. Whatever the reason may be, I believe it to be the fact that our universities don't often find a way unaided to break down the barriers between different institutions or even between different departments in the same institution. University administration for one thing is proverbially stingy in giving professors a chance to move about. When men from different institutions do get together, it is usually at the expense of one of the foundations, and I don't think their money is often used to better advantage. It is from such contacts that the co-operative research projects, which, as I said a moment ago, are characteristic of our day, usually arise.

The university, on the other hand, helps the foundation where it most needs help. " Where shall wisdom be found and where is the place of understanding? " I refer more particularly to the wisdom we seek rather than to the wisdom which is offered to us unsolicited. It is no easy thing for the ear of a foundation to recognize and to understand the still small voice, with all the loud-speakers which are trained upon it. The job of a foundation executive, I may say in passing, is a hazardous one, particularly as regards character depreciation. University presidents are said to have the same trouble, but I doubt if they have it to the same degree. It can't be good for a man to have all his jokes laughed at and all his opinions, regardless of their validity, immediately concurred in. There is only one exception. The importance and practicability of making the grant about which the visitor has called is not open to debate.

So closely are the universities and foundations related in objectives and in the individuals or teams at work upon the realization of these objectives, that when the universities ask us to speak of our opportunities and dangers, we can reply that in a general way our opportunities are their opportunities; our dangers to a very considerable degree their dangers. I am, of course, using the term university in its broadest sense, as covering everything contributing to the advancement of knowledge, whether carried forward in a degree-granting institution or in a school system or in a separate institution.

The opportunities seem to lie rather in helping specific undertakings previously approved by a representative group of qualified persons, rather than in contributions to the general purposes of individual institutions. Alumni and other generously minded individuals can look after the latter, but the former fall into the category of things that everybody will endorse but that no one seems to think it is his business to pay for.

82

From the nature of its organization and its contacts, often from the very fact that its activities are not limited to the rigidly academic, the foundation itself is sometimes the first to see a need. In exceptional cases, the best opportunity for the foundation and the best service to the university lies in direct and vigorous opposition to the prevailing academic point of view. An example is the campaign on medical education, started by a report of the Carnegie Foundation and continued for a decade by the General Education Board. I don't mean that the opposition has lasted for ten years, but it is certainly true that proceedings began, in the words of Mrs. Malaprop, " with a little aversion."

If a foundation man had selected it, I think the title of this symposium might well have been " The Opportunities, Dangers and Dilemmas of the Foundation," because in the day's work we don't have much time to think either of the first or the second, but we constantly have to choose as to which horn of the third we shall cling. The old questions of line *vs.* staff, quantity *vs.* quality, concentration *vs.* diffusion, complete *vs.* divided responsibility, all find characteristic ways of presenting themselves in our calling. If, for example, a foundation maintains its own operating staff, up goes the overhead and in comes the danger of slipping into routine-ism. If we farm out our projects, we have divided responsibility, delays and misunderstandings. Personally, as a democrat with a small d, I believe in so doing, but the actual results are often maddening. What the foundations, like the police, call an inside job, is much the simplest to carry through.

Or take the choice between a limited objective and a willingness to follow any promising lead. The former makes for continuity of policy and cumulative results. On the other hand, once in so often a long shot brings down big game. The Toronto grant which produced insulin is a good case in point.

What should be the relations of the foundations to one another? There are those who see in a close co-operation, if not a conspiracy in restraint of trade, at any rate the possibility of an undue concentration. If there is no co-operation, on the other hand, there is the danger of duplication of effort, of working at cross-purposes and the very real chance of being whipsawed by one of the adroit professional money-raisers, whose tribe has increased so rapidly in recent years.

Then there is the choice between the advantage of such complete responsibility for an enterprise as is undertaken in the making of a non-conditional grant, as against a larger total amount available for the purpose in question, resulting from a gift made conditionally upon the raising of a stated sum from other sources. Much can be said in favor of each of them. Each method has its advantages and its drawbacks, and one of the foundation groups, namely the Rockefeller, usually makes its grants upon a conditional basis, whereas the Carnegie grants are likely to be unrestricted.

It is, I think, fortunate that there is no uniformity as to these questions of foundation policy, and fortunate also that there is not always consistency of practice, for after all the modern foundation as a social instrument is still in the experimental stage, and we need much more experience before venturing on anything beyond the most tentative body of doctrine regarding it.

The foregoing, by the way, applies to my own expressions of opinion this afternoon. Perhaps I ought to say at this point that a few days ago I went over my notes with one of my Carnegie colleagues; and without going into details I may as well confess that if the committee had happened to ask him here instead of me, you would have had a somewhat different contribution.

Now, not forgetting what I have just said, let us

consider the dangers, imaginary and real. Not so long ago we used to hear that the grants of the foundations would dry up the springs of individual philanthropy. This has not proved to be the case. Indeed, I should be rather inclined to think that the danger, if any, is that conditional grants from foundations sometimes overstimulate gifts which individuals are not really justified in making.

There is a real danger, as many of us believe, in accelerating to the point of distortion what would otherwise be the normal evolution of an idea or a project. In other words, generous foundation grants sometimes make things too simple. An enterprise is put upon Easy Street long before it is for the best interest of itself or of mankind to have it reach that well-paved highway. Of course, it is all a matter of degree. We no longer believe in artificially hardening our children by Spartan rigors, but the danger of going too far in the other direction is not a fanciful one.

These, however, are incidental matters, and can be controlled by intelligent administration. Some underlying questions, on the other hand, can not be so easily disposed of. There are those who believe, and their numbers are not negligible, that a grave danger to the community lies in the inevitable growth of foundations in numbers and power until an undue proportion of our total wealth is tied up in bodies which apparently have been devised with great skill to be free from control either by public opinion or by due process of law. Such disquietude is not without some historical justification, for in the time of Henry VIII half the wealth of England lay in the foundations of that day, which were, of course, the religious foundations; and the Reformation in England was concerned quite as much with getting at these repositories of wealth as with any theological considerations. In his report as acting president of the Carnegie Corporation for 1923, Dr. Henry S. Pritchett has included an important historical study of foundations and their works and has shown how blind the custodians of these funds have often been to the public interest, and how often, even when they wished to do the right thing, they were prevented by the rigidity of their trust.

With respect to our situation to-day, however, certain factors should be borne in mind. In the first place, in six of the eight large foundations which concern themselves with education, the capital funds are not tied up in perpetuity. The trustees may at any time distribute not only the interest but the principal. Technically speaking, I suppose, they are not foundations at all. This freedom was first bestowed upon a board of trustees by the charter of the Russell Sage Foundation in 1907. It has been extended to those in control of the three great Rockefeller funds — the Rockefeller Foundation, the General Education Board and the Laura Spelman Rockefeller Memorial — and also to the Milbank and Commonwealth Funds. If therefore the trustees of these funds should at any time recognize the existence of the danger of undue concentration, they can quickly meet it.

In the second place, I, for one, believe that the number of very large foundations is not likely to be greatly increased in the future. Those which we now have are the fruits of an economic and financial situation which has already changed. The individuals or family groups which could, if they would, found hundred million dollar endowments, do not exceed ten or a dozen at the outset. Income taxes, death duties, perhaps changing standards in the business and the industrial world, have already operated to limit the number of huge fortunes, and consequently huge foundations. On the other hand, endowments for specific purposes, with relatively smaller capitalization, for example the John Simon Guggenheim Memorial Foundation, are likely to increase rapidly in number; and

I believe we can look forward also to the growth, both in number and capitalization, of community trusts. From the diversified nature of their objectives in the case of the first type, and from the geographical limitations in the case of the second, these organizations do not present the same problem as would an increase in the large endowments for general purposes.

What lies behind the fear of the concentration of great funds in the control of a comparatively small number of people is of course the possibility that the income from funds of this size may be so directed as ultimately to create a nation-wide limitation upon the freedom of human thought and human action. It should be added, therefore, that certain men and women who feel no alarm as to undue concentration are nevertheless apprehensive as to the future. They fear, not a deliberate attempt at control, but rather an unconscious limitation of the field of foundation interests and activities through a limitation of the angle of vision of those in control. The trustees originally chosen are, they say, conservatives, and, naturally enough, because the fiduciary responsibility of these boards is an essential part of their job, and those competent by training to handle large sums of money are pretty sure to be conservatives. As vacancies occur, they will inevitably be filled, in the opinion of these doubters, by others of the same stripe. As to the safeguarding of the funds, this is all right, but as to the distribution of income, in other words, as to the program of the foundation, is it the experience of mankind that the ideas upon which future progress depends are welcome to those who are satisfied with things as they are?

It is a fair question, and a question of which a good many of the members of the existing boards are perfectly cognizant, in spite of their conservatism. They are all looking for younger people to fill vacancies, and this in itself involves a shift of the centre of gravity toward what we call the left. They sometimes consciously seek a man with whom they know they will disagree on most points. A procedure which minimizes the danger of an ingrown board is now the accepted order in the community trusts, and these are destined, I think, to take an increasingly important place in the picture as time goes on. These trusts divide their responsibility, the custody and investment of funds being in the hands of professional bankers, the distribution of income in the hands of a separate group, not self-perpetuating. In the case of the New York Community Trust, for example, this group consists of eleven people, six of the eleven mem-

bers, a majority, being nominated respectively by
the senior judge of the United States Circuit Court
of Appeals of the Second District, by the president
of the Chamber of Commerce of the State of New
York, by the president of the Brooklyn Institute
of Arts and Sciences, the mayor of the City of New
York, the president of the Academy of Medicine
and the president of the Association of the Bar.
In this connection, it should be remembered that
five of the twelve persons now composing the
Board of the Carnegie Corporation are members
by virtue of holding the presidencies of the Carnegie Endowment for International Peace, the Foundation for the Advancement of Teaching, the Hero
Fund Commission, the Carnegie Institute of Pitts-
burgh and the Carnegie Institution of Washington. In all, 115 persons share the responsibility
for their selection. Of course, Mr. Carnegie had a
special purpose in making this provision, but it has
not been a bad thing for the Corporation all along
the line of its activities.

I hazard the prophecy that the years to come
will find, let us call it a greater variety of light and
shade in the makeup of the foundation boards, and
I also venture to predict that this will make no
particular difference in their policies and programs,
but that it will have an important effect by in-

creasing public confidence, a point to which I shall return in a moment.

In my opinion, the real danger lies, not in concentration of wealth, or in conservatism or radicalism, but in a misunderstanding of function. Danger arises whenever any group with power in its hands, whether it be a state legislature, or the board of a university or of a foundation, believes it to be its business to use its power to direct opinion. Any such group is a dangerous group, regardless of the manner of its makeup and regardless of whether its action is conscious or unconscious, and, if conscious, whether benign or sinister in purpose.

Let me add that a comparison of the programs of the foundations say of five years ago and of today will, I think, show that the foundations themselves are coming to have a progressively clearer understanding as to the distinction between the advancement of knowledge and the direction of opinion.

After all, the fundamental safeguard against the unsocial use of these funds lies, in the long run, in public opinion and the possibility of public control. The apparent immunity of those who direct them lies in the freedom from taxation which the foundations enjoy, but there is nothing irrevocable about the present exemption of such bodies, and the community, if at any time it felt so disposed, could tax an offending foundation, or all foundations, out of active existence. The Supreme Court, in Veazie Bank *vs.* Fenno, years ago set a precedent for the use of the tax power for purposes other than revenue. The element of public confidence in the makeup of foundation boards is therefore of very practical importance. Even more important is as wide an understanding as possible of what the foundations do and how they do it.

If I may be permitted to refer for a moment to the recent action at Madison: the point of importance in my judgment is not that the university should or should not receive financial aid from a foundation, but that nine citizens of a great commonwealth, selected presumably because of their understanding of educational developments and educational problems, should feel that by voting as they did they were carrying out the trust imposed upon them as regents. Is not this an evidence that wider opportunities should be given to the public to understand something of the actual steps by which the trustees of an American educational foundation endeavor to carry out the trust imposed *on them?* It is hard to conceive that a fair-minded man or woman who studied the day by day operations of any one of the important educational foundations should fail to realize that the broadly co-operative character of these operations offers the most effective safeguard, if safeguard were needed, against any employment of these trust funds based upon unworthy motives.

The foundations make mistakes both of omission and of commission, and in this imperfect world, they will continue to do so. The real test of their utility lies in their record of positive accomplishment. Let me give in closing just two examples of such accomplishment. In the first place, no history of American education would be complete without recognition of the responsibility of the General Education Board for the improvement of secondary education all through our southern states. Secondly, the story of human progress through the quarter century just closing would not be told, no matter how briefly, without reference to what the Rockefeller Foundation has done for public health throughout the world. Personally, I think the foundations may safely rest their case on these two pieces of evidence.